Children's Food Advertisement

Children's Food Advertisement

Refreshing Drinks

Advertisements for Women

Advertisements for Women

Advertisements for Men

Advertisements for Men

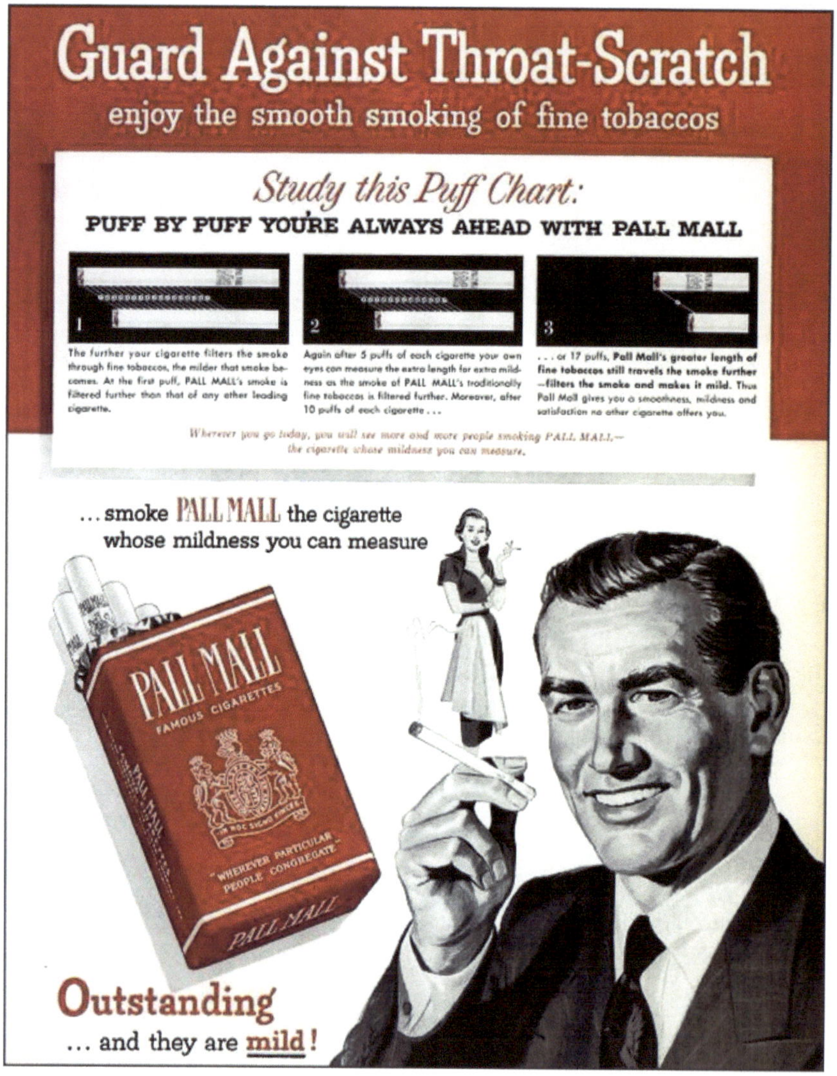

Guard Against Throat-Scratch

enjoy the smooth smoking of fine tobaccos

Study this Puff Chart:

PUFF BY PUFF YOU'RE ALWAYS AHEAD WITH PALL MALL

1 The further your cigarette filters the smoke through fine tobaccos, the milder that smoke becomes. At the first puff, PALL MALL's smoke is filtered further than that of any other leading cigarette.

2 Again after 5 puffs of each cigarette your own eyes can measure the extra length for extra mildness as the smoke of PALL MALL's traditionally fine tobaccos is filtered further. Moreover, after 10 puffs of each cigarette . . .

3 . . . or 17 puffs, **Pall Mall's greater length of fine tobaccos still travels the smoke further —filters the smoke and makes it mild.** Thus Pall Mall gives you a smoothness, mildness and satisfaction no other cigarette offers you.

Wherever you go today, you will see more and more people smoking PALL MALL— the cigarette whose mildness you can measure.

. . . smoke PALL MALL the cigarette whose mildness you can measure

PALL MALL
FAMOUS CIGARETTES
IN HOC SIGNO VINCES
"WHEREVER PARTICULAR PEOPLE CONGREGATE"
PALL MALL

Outstanding

. . . and they are mild!

Best Cars

Cadillac

Ford Thunderbird

Best Cars

Packard

Mercury

Icons and Celebrities

Dwight D. Eisenhower

Richard Nixon

Icons and Celebrities

Marilyn Monroe

Elvis Presley

RCA
VICTOR
STEREO EFFECT REPROCESSED FROM MONOPHONIC
ELVIS
PRESLEY

Petrol Pumps

Ampol Service Station

Petrol Pumps

Aero Motors, Murray Street

Diners

PCHarrisburg-LV-Midway Diner

Diners

Strongbow Turkey Inn and Farm
Valparaiso, Indiana

Restaurants

Space Needle Restaurant
Seattle, Washington

Restaurants

KINGFISH Restaurant
Treasure Island Florida

Cafeteria

SCHENSUL'S CAFETERIA
Kalamazoo MI

Cafeteria

DRIFTWOOD CAFETERIA
St. Petersburg FL

Kitchen Styles

Kitchen Styles

Kitchen Styles

Living Room Décor

Living Room Décor

Living Room Décor

Families

Families

Families

Motels

Catalina Motel Kentucky

Motels

TRAVEL INN MOTEL New Orleans Louisiana

Motels

FERNWOOD MOTEL, Bushkill Pennsylvania

Schools

Schools

Schools

Supermarket

Appliances

Just TOUCH AND GO
lightly!
IBM
CLEAR
SET
RETURN
SHIFT
IBM
Electric Typewriters

Appliances

Appliances

BAUSCH & LOMB BALOMATIC

Thanksgiving

Dinner Table

Christmas

Silver tree Christmas

Gifts

Acknowledgement

Page No. I Author/s I Title I Source I License

Children's Foods Ads (Hi Ho Crackers) I 1950sUnlimited
Hi Ho Crackers 1951 I https://www.flickr.com/photos/blakta2/8214341266/
Attribution 2.0 Generic (CC BY 2.0)

Children's Foods Ads (Karo Syrup) I 1950sUnlimited
Karo Syrup 1955 I https://www.flickr.com/photos/blakta2/8222618239/
Attribution 2.0 Generic (CC BY 2.0)

Children's Foods Ads (Sunkist) I 1950sUnlimited
Sunkist Oranges 1953 I https://www.flickr.com/photos/blakta2/8214498377/
Attribution 2.0 Generic (CC BY 2.0)

Children's Foods Ads (POST Sugar crisp cereals) I 1950sUnlimited
POST sugar crisp cereal 1955 I https://www.flickr.com/photos/blakta2/8222629065/
Attribution 2.0 Generic (CC BY 2.0)

Refreshing Drinks (Coke) I 1950sUnlimited
Coke 1954 I https://www.flickr.com/photos/blakta2/8209857715/
Attribution 2.0 Generic (CC BY 2.0)

Refreshing Drinks (7Up) I 1950sUnlimited
7 UP cola 1951 I https://www.flickr.com/photos/blakta2/8213256599/
Attribution 2.0 Generic (CC BY 2.0)

Ads Targeted for Women I 1950sUnlimited
Lustre Creme featuring Esther Williams I https://www.flickr.com/photos/blakta2/8215554946/
Attribution 2.0 Generic (CC BY 2.0)

Ads Targeted for Women I 1950sUnlimited
Community Silverware 1953 illustrated by Jon Whitcomb I https://www.flickr.com/photos/blakta2/8215698878/
Attribution 2.0 Generic (CC BY 2.0)

Ads Targeted for Women I 1950sUnlimited
Crosley Electric Range 1953 I https://www.flickr.com/photos/blakta2/8215716112/
Attribution 2.0 Generic (CC BY 2.0)

Ads Targeted for Women I 1950sUnlimited
Bliss Home Permanent 1957 I https://www.flickr.com/photos/blakta2/8222500732/
Attribution 2.0 Generic (CC BY 2.0)

Ads Targetted for Men I 1950sUnlimited
McGregor sportswear 1955 I https://www.flickr.com/photos/blakta2/8223724152/
Attribution 2.0 Generic (CC BY 2.0)

Ads Targeted for Men I 1950sUnlimited
Ballentine Ale 1953 I https://www.flickr.com/photos/blakta2/8215666654/
Attribution 2.0 Generic (CC BY 2.0)

Ads Targeted for Men I 1950sUnlimited
Vaseline Hair Tonic 1951 I https://www.flickr.com/photos/blakta2/8214333782/
Attribution 2.0 Generic (CC BY 2.0)

Ads Targeted for Men I 1950sUnlimited
Pal Mall Cigarettes 1951 I https://www.flickr.com/photos/blakta2/8214342568/
Attribution 2.0 Generic (CC BY 2.0)

1956 Cadillac I Matthew Paul Argall
1956 Cadillac I https://www.flickr.com/photos/79157069@N03/46441731324/
Attribution 2.0 Generic (CC BY 2.0)

Packard I Txemari (Argazki)
Packard en estación de servicio, años 1950s I https://www.flickr.com/photos/serrvill/47682072041/
Public Domain Mark 1.0

1955 Thunderbird I David Berry
1955 Thunderbird I https://www.flickr.com/photos/dberry/6602088549/
Attribution 2.0 Generic (CC BY 2.0)

1954 Mercury I David Berry
1954 Mercury I https://www.flickr.com/photos/dberry/6602086483/
Attribution 2.0 Generic (CC BY 2.0)

Dwight D. Eisenhower I Marion Doss General
Dwight D. Eisenhower, Supreme Allied Commander I https://www.flickr.com/photos/ooocha/2629711007/
Attribution-ShareAlike 2.0 Generic (CC BY-SA 2.0)

Richard Nixon I Rupert Colley (historyinanhour)
Richard Nixon I https://www.flickr.com/photos/historyinanhour/4775027305/
Attribution 2.0 Generic (CC BY 2.0)

Elvis Presley I brett jordan
Elvis Presley I https://www.flickr.com/photos/x1brett/8341828429/
Attribution 2.0 Generic (CC BY 2.0)

Marilyn Monroe I Rokr Rafterson
Marilyn Monroe I https://www.flickr.com/photos/raftrokr/430039842/
Attribution 2.0 Generic (CC BY 2.0)

Ampol Service Station I Blue Mountains Library, Local Studies
Ampol Service Station I https://www.flickr.com/photos/blue_mountains_library_-_local_studies/51222823972/
Attribution-ShareAlike 2.0 Generic (CC BY-SA 2.0)

1950s Aero Motors I Gawler History
Murray Street 153 c1950 I https://www.flickr.com/photos/gawler_history/8117955819/
Attribution-ShareAlike 2.0 Generic (CC BY-SA 2.0)

1950s Diner I Peachhead
PCHarrisburg-LV-MidwayDiner I https://www.flickr.com/photos/peachhead/24193626410/
Public Domain Mark 1.0

1950s Diner I Steve Shook I Strongbow Turkey Inn and Farm, circa 1950s - Valparaiso, Indiana
https://www.flickr.com/photos/shookphotos/4182397179/
Attribution 2.0 Generic (CC BY 2.0)

Restaurants I 1950sUnlimited
Space Needle Restaurant, Seattle, Washington I https://www.flickr.com/photos/blakta2/8543542699/
Attribution 2.0 Generic (CC BY 2.0)

Restaurants I 1950sUnlimited
KINGFISH RESTAURANT treasure island florida I https://www.flickr.com/photos/blakta2/8549256279/
Attribution 2.0 Generic (CC BY 2.0)

Cafetaria I 1950sUnlimited
SCHENSUL'S CAFETERIA RESTAURANT Kalamazoo MI I https://www.flickr.com/photos/blakta2/8552926380/
Attribution 2.0 Generic (CC BY 2.0)

Cafetaria I 1950sUnlimited
DRIFTWOOD CAFETERIA RESTAURANT St. Petersburg FL I https://www.flickr.com/photos/blakta2/8553075715/
Attribution 2.0 Generic (CC BY 2.0)

Kitchen Styles I Ethan
https://www.flickr.com/photos/42353480@N02/5764405142/
Attribution 2.0 Generic (CC BY 2.0)

Kitchen Styles I Ethan
https://www.flickr.com/photos/42353480@N02/5757760150/
Attribution 2.0 Generic (CC BY 2.0)

Kitchen Styles I Ethan
https://www.flickr.com/photos/42353480@N02/5763854931/
Attribution 2.0 Generic (CC BY 2.0)

Living Room I 1950sUnlimited
Detail Hibriten Chairs Koylon Foam Cushioning 1954 I https://www.flickr.com/photos/blakta2/8566929119/
Attribution 2.0 Generic (CC BY 2.0)

Living Room I Deidre Woollard
1950s sofa I https://www.flickr.com/photos/deidrew/5040944712/
Attribution 2.0 Generic (CC BY 2.0)

Living Room I Craig Howell I Jeff street living room, 1952
https://www.flickr.com/photos/seat850/2687638303/
Attribution 2.0 Generic (CC BY 2.0)

Families I cmun_Project
1-Family Time I https://www.flickr.com/photos/62274237@N06/5663134445/
Attribution 2.0 Generic (CC BY 2.0)

Families I Seattle Municipal Archives
W.H. Shumard family, circa 1955 I https://www.flickr.com/photos/seattlemunicipalarchives/4167079112/
Attribution 2.0 Generic (CC BY 2.0)

Families I daves_archive_1
img011 I https://www.flickr.com/photos/foundin_a_attic/31868847424/
Attribution 2.0 Generic (CC BY 2.0)

Motels I 1950sUnlimited
Catalina Motel Kentucky I https://www.flickr.com/photos/blakta2/8538069859/
Attribution 2.0 Generic (CC BY 2.0)

Motels I 1950sUnlimited
TRAVEL INN MOTEL New Orleans Louisiana I https://www.flickr.com/photos/blakta2/8539205514/
Attribution 2.0 Generic (CC BY 2.0)

Motels I 1950sUnlimited
FERNWOOD MOTEL, Bushkill Pennsylvania I https://www.flickr.com/photos/blakta2/8512561388/
Attribution 2.0 Generic (CC BY 2.0)

Schools I daves_archive_1
kodachrome red 1950s slides I https://www.flickr.com/photos/foundin_a_attic/47228240992/
Attribution 2.0 Generic (CC BY 2.0)

Schools I Don Graham
San Timoteo Canyon Schoolhouse, CA 3-4-17a I https://www.flickr.com/photos/23155134@N06/33227164186/
Attribution-ShareAlike 2.0 Generic (CC BY-SA 2.0)

Schools I Seattle Municipal Archives
Students and teachers at Newhalem School, 1954 I https://www.flickr.com/photos/seattlemunicipalarchives/31061165815/
Attribution 2.0 Generic (CC BY 2.0)

Supermarket I Seattle Municipal Archives
Supermarket interior, 1955 I https://www.flickr.com/photos/seattlemunicipalarchives/9969632573/
Attribution 2.0 Generic (CC BY 2.0)

Typewriter I 1950sUnlimited
IBM 1952 I https://www.flickr.com/photos/blakta2/8080800505/
Attribution 2.0 Generic (CC BY 2.0)

Vacuum Cleaner I 1950sUnlimited
ELECTRO I https://www.flickr.com/photos/blakta2/8080786235/
Attribution 2.0 Generic (CC BY 2.0)

Balomatic I 1950sUnlimited
Bausch & Lomb 1958 I https://www.flickr.com/photos/blakta2/8256150085/
Attribution 2.0 Generic (CC BY 2.0)

Fridge I 1950sUnlimited
1948KELVINATOR I https://www.flickr.com/photos/blakta2/8205072109/
Attribution 2.0 Generic (CC BY 2.0)

Thanksgiving (Dinner table) I Brian Crawford
Family Dinner I https://www.flickr.com/photos/crawfordbrian/31057872102/
Attribution-ShareAlike 2.0 Generic (CC BY-SA 2.0)

Christmas (Silver Christmas) I Steven Miller
(Sam Howzit) I Silver Christmas Tree https://www.flickr.com/photos/aloha75/16480619526/
Attribution 2.0 Generic (CC BY 2.0)

Christmas (gifts) I daves_archive_1
1950s red slides I https://www.flickr.com/photos/foundin_a_attic/31890306273/
Attribution 2.0 Generic (CC BY 2.0)

www.ingramcontent.com/pod-product-compliance
Ingram Content Group UK Ltd.
Pitfield, Milton Keynes, MK11 3LW, UK
UKHW060111300726
14090UKWH00002B/138

* 9 7 8 9 1 8 9 4 5 2 8 0 0 *